SMYTHE GAMBRELL
LIBRARY

Caroline Robinson '98

PRESENTED BY

The Westminster Schools
With grateful appreciation to
Mr. & Mrs. Eric P. Berezin
for outstanding volunteer support
to the 1997-98 Annual Fund

WESTMINSTER SCHOOLS

A M E R I C A N   T R A I L S

THE ROYAL ROADS
Spanish Trails in North America

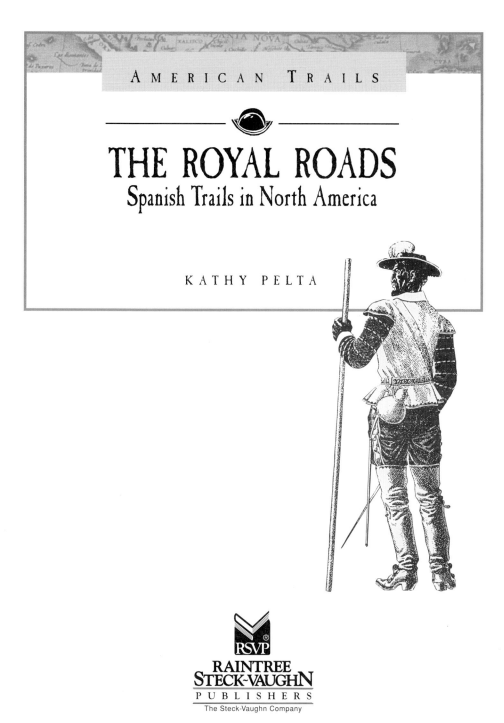

AMERICAN TRAILS

THE ROYAL ROADS
Spanish Trails in North America

KATHY PELTA

RSVP
RAINTREE
STECK-VAUGHN
PUBLISHERS
The Steck-Vaughn Company

Austin, Texas

Published by Raintree Steck-Vaughn Publishers, an imprint of Steck-Vaughn Company

Raintree Steck-Vaughn Publishers Staff

Publishing Director: Walter Kossmann   Project Manager: Lyda Guz
Editor: Shirley Shalit   Electronic Production: Scott Melcer
Photo Editor: Margie Foster

Library of Congress Cataloging-in-Publication Data
Pelta, Kathy.
    The royal roads : Spanish trails in North America / by Kathy Pelta.
        p.   cm.– (American trails)
    Includes bibliographical references and index.
    Summary: Describes the development and use of many of the major trails established by Spanish soldiers, traders, and priests in Mexico, the Southwest, and Florida between the 1500s and the 1800s.
    ISBN 0-8172-4074-8
    1. North America – Discovery and exploration – Spanish – Juvenile literature.
2. Trails – Southwest, New – History – Juvenile literature.   3. Trails – Florida – History – Juvenile literature.   4. Southwest, New – History – To 1848 – Juvenile literature.   5. Florida – History – To 1821 – Juvenile literature.   [1. North America – Discovery and exploration – Spanish.   2. Trails – Southwest, New – History.   3. Trails – Florida – History.   4. Southwest, New – History – To 1848.   5. Florida – History – To 1821.]   I. Title.   II. Series: Pelta, Kathy. American trails.
E123.P415   1997   96-37369
970.01'6 – dc21   CIP   AC

Printed and bound in the United States

1 2 3 4 5 6 7 8 9 0 LB 00 99 98 97

Acknowledgments

The author and publisher would like to thank the following for photos and illustrations. Cover (inset) The Granger Collection, (map) Westlight; p. 3 University of Texas, Institute of Texan Cultures, San Antonio; pp. 7, 11, 14, 17, 20, 26, 27 North Wind Picture Archives; p. 29 Corbis-Bettmann; p. 30 University of Texas, Institute of Texan Cultures, San Antonio; p. 31 Courtesy St. Augustine Historical Society Collection; p. 33 North Wind Picture Archive; p. 35 Florida State Archives; p. 36 The Granger Collection; p. 43 Courtesy Texas Highways; p. 45 North Wind Picture Archives; p. 46 Courtesy Texas Highways; p. 48 The Granger Collection; p. 50 Courtesy Natchitoches Parish Trust Commission; pp. 51, 57 North Wind Picture Archives; p. 58 Courtesy Texas State Archives; p. 59 Popperfoto/Archive Photos; p. 61 The Bancroft Library, University of California Berkeley; p. 62 Arizona Office of Tourism; p. 63 Arizona Historical Society Library; p. 65 The Granger Collection; p. 66 (both) North Wind Picture Archives; p. 67 © Superstock; p. 68 Southwest Museum, Los Angeles Photo #22.G.978Q; p. 70 KEAN/Archive Photos; p. 71 North Wind Picture Archives; p. 75 Corbis-Bettmann; pp. 76, 79 (both) Courtesy The Old Mission Church, Los Angeles; p. 82 (top right) © Ken Laffal; pp. 83, 84 North Wind Picture Archives.

Cartography: GeoSystems, Inc.

Contents:

North American Trails

There were trails winding through the woods and wilderness of North America long before any Europeans arrived. Some paths were shortcuts that animals took to salt licks or favorite water holes. Native Americans used these paths or created their own as they hunted and gathered food, traded with neighbors, and made pilgrimages to sacred sites.

The first Europeans to explore North America usually followed established trails. Sometimes, with the help of native guides, they blazed new ones. After the explorers came soldiers and missionaries, traders and trappers, and—eventually—settlers. Gradually, favorite trails were widened to accommodate oxcarts and horse-drawn wagons, then stagecoaches, and finally, motorcars. Some trails became routes for railroad lines.

The trails that criss-crossed the United States reflected its history. In the east, soldiers and traders and farmers used the trails that woodsmen blazed between settled areas and the frontier inland. Over trails in the southwest, cattle ranchers moved their herds from Texas to northern markets and rail centers in the Great Plains. Beyond the Mississippi, trails to the far west beckoned travelers of every kind—from adventurers and prospectors to religious groups and homesteaders seeking better lives for their families.

This book deals with the trails established by the Spanish in the southeast, the southwest, and along the California coast. These Spanish trails linked Catholic missions, military posts, and pueblos (towns) built between the 1500s and the 1800s, when Spain claimed much of what is now the United States.

For God, Glory, and Gold!

I n 1519, some 27 years after Christopher Columbus first landed in the New World, Hernando Cortés sailed from the West Indies to find gold in what is now Mexico. In two years his small army had plundered and subdued the ancient empire of the Aztecs. The Spanish conquerors claimed the Aztecs' vast treasury of gold and jewels and destroyed the Aztec capital, Tenochtitlán. In its place they created a new capital city they called Mexico. What had once been the mighty Aztec empire became the Spanish

Aztecs greet Hernando Cortés as he leads his army into the city of Cholula on his march to Tenochtitlán, capital of the Aztec empire.

colony of New Spain. Hernando Cortés had a magnificent palace built for himself from which he would rule as New Spain's governor.

Inspired by the success of Cortés, other Spanish *conquistadores*—or conquerors—went on to defeat other Native American civilizations and seek more gold. In 1531, Francisco Pizarro led a few soldiers from what is now Panama south into Peru. There Pizarro conquered the Incas, a people even wealthier than the Aztecs.

But farther north—in what is now the United States—the early conquerors found no treasure, although rumors

The Royal Notary's Pronouncement: Agree, or Else

A royal notary—the Spanish king's representative who prepared legal papers and administered oaths—always accompanied the Spanish conquerors. As the native people gathered to greet the invaders of their land, it was the notary's duty to read to them—in Spanish—from an official document stating that in 1493 the pope had made Spain legal owner of any lands discovered in the Western Hemisphere. Therefore, the native people were told, they had to "yield themselves to the Spanish crown and accept the preaching of Christianity." If the people agreed, nothing would happen. If the people resisted, the Spanish felt they had the legal right to "impose their will with fire and sword." In other words, they could enslave or even kill any of the Native Americans—whom the Spaniards called "Indians"—who refused to convert to Christianity. Unfortunately for the Indians, they spoke no Spanish and could not understand a word of what was being said.

spread that somewhere in the New World there were vast collections of gold. Some native people had even hinted that somewhere inland were seven cities built of gold. As early as 1513 Ponce de León searched in vain in Florida for gold and pearls (and, some say, the "Fountain of Youth"). Nearly three decades later, in 1539, Hernando De Soto led his soldiers on a futile treasure hunt that also began in Florida. With him traveled Catholic priests who were to explain Christianity to the native people. For by this time, the king of Spain had decreed that the main purpose of discovering new lands was not to conquer, but rather to save the natives by helping them become Christians.

Like Ponce de León, Hernando De Soto never discovered any riches, though he explored as far west as what are now Arkansas, Louisiana, and Texas. Meanwhile, Francisco Coronado had crossed the range of mountains west of Mexico City. Then he headed up the coast to find those fabled cities of gold he had heard about. Before giving up his search, Coronado and his army passed the Grand Canyon and reached as far north as the present state of Kansas.

Although these early Spaniards did not find in North America the gold and jewels they sought so desperately, they brought their Spanish king a far greater treasure: a colony more vast than Spain itself. Besides present-day Mexico, New Spain eventually included all or part of the Florida peninsula, Texas, New Mexico, Arizona, Utah, Colorado, and California.

By three hundred years later, Spain had given up nearly all of its claims to land in North America. But for the people of the United States, an important Spanish legacy remained: the network of trailways that spanned the new nation.

ONE

El Camino Real: Mexico to New Mexico

When the Spanish invaded the Aztec empire and made it a colony of New Spain, they did so in the name of their king. Each trail that led from Mexico City, the capital of New Spain, to one of the colony's outposts was called *El Camino Real*. These Spanish words mean "the king's highway" or "the royal road."

From Mexico City to the east, a *camino real* wound across the mountains to Veracruz, the fortress on the Gulf of Mexico built by the Spanish *conquistador* Hernando Cortés. From here Cortés began his invasion of the Aztec empire. After the conquest of the Aztecs, this royal road was the route followed by all who traveled between Mexico City and the gulf. Later, other royal roads led southwest from Mexico City to Acapulco on the Pacific Coast and to San Salvador in Central America.

A *camino real* heading north from Mexico City was started in the early 1540s, after prospectors found silver at Querétaro on a plateau between two mountain ranges about 100 miles from the capital. At first, it was little more than a rough path. To reach Querétaro by oxcart over this royal road took two weeks.

Three hundred miles farther north, at Zacatecas, prospectors found the greatest silver lodes of all in 1546.

10

A silver rush began. Soon mines dotted the hills and valleys. The northbound *camino real* was quickly extended to this region. It was used mostly by pack mules that brought supplies in to the mines and hauled silver out. But in a short time the mule trains shared the royal road with traders, government officials, Spanish priests, and settlers moving to the area.

Despite the hardships of living so far from Mexico City and concerns about safety, many Spaniards chose to settle around Zacatecas. They operated silver mines, with the Native Americans providing the labor. Others, with the help of Indian servants, started farms or ranches to raise cattle and crops to feed the growing community. Garrisons were built to house soldiers, whose job was to protect the

From a seventeenth century engraving, a cutaway view of Indian slaves digging inside a Zacatecas silver mine. Some workers carry torches to provide light.

Early *caminos reales* from Mexico City led east to Veracruz, southwest to Acapulco, south to San Salvador in Central America, and north to Querétaro, Zacatecas, and Santa Barbara. By 1598, Oñate (see page 15) had extended the northern *camino real* across the Rio Grande to the Spanish colony at Santa Fe in Nueva (New) Mexico.

Spanish people—and also to oversee Indian slaves who were forced to mine the silver ore.

Since the northbound *camino real* cut through the homeland of the Chichimeca people, the Chichimeca often staged raids against these newcomers who were trespassing on their land. To guard travelers on the road against possible attack, Spanish authorities set up military forts and garrisons at key points along the way. Often visitors to the mining region also banded together in large caravans, and hired soldiers as escorts.

In the barren hills and dusty plains beyond Zacatecas, prospectors discovered more silver, and also gold, rubies, and iron ore. So the *camino real* was extended. By 1564, it reached 850 miles north of Mexico City, to the settlement of Santa Barbara (in Mexico, not California).

For the next 20 years, the frontier of New Spain—or Mexico, as it came to be called—remained at the small mining town of Santa Barbara. Beyond this point, no royal road existed. There was nothing but desert from the Conchos River, just north of Santa Barbara, to the Rio Grande that now separates Mexico from the United States. Except for slave-hunters, few Spaniards ventured into this desolate area. Despite a law against taking Indian slaves, some Spaniards continued to raid native villages and seize the native people to work in the mines. The slave-hunters simply claimed the Indians were attacking them, therefore it was legal for the Spaniards to take them prisoner.

Late in the 1500s, an Indian servant in Santa Barbara told his priest, Father Agustín Rodríguez, about a Native American farming group in the far north. He said the people of this group, called Pueblos, were expert weavers and pottery makers. Father Rodríguez wanted to find out more about the Pueblos, and so he asked for permission to go north. At that time the people in the Spanish colony could not travel beyond the frontier without government approval.

Permission was granted, and Father Rodríguez began to assemble trade goods for his journey. For besides converting the Pueblos to Christianity, the priest hoped to trade with them. In exchange for the Pueblos' fine blankets and clay pots he would offer them colored beads, red caps, and

Painting on the wall of a kiva (Indian ceremonial chamber) in a Pueblo village in present-day New Mexico. Spanish priests came here in the 1500s to convert the Pueblos to the Roman Catholic religion.

hawkbells—small, round bells with a metal pellet inside that Spanish bird trainers sometimes fastened to the legs of hawks they used for hunting.

In 1581 Father Rodríguez set out with two other priests, 16 Indian servants, and a few horses and goats. Nine soldiers went along as escorts. To avoid the harsh desert Father Rodríguez and his company angled northeast and stayed close to rivers. At each night's stop, they erected a cross. When the group reached the mighty river they called Rio del Norte, and we now call Rio Grande, they followed it north. At the first Pueblo village, the soldiers—feeling that their escorting job was done—turned and started back to Santa Barbara. But the priests refused to leave. They chose instead to stay to preach the word of God to the Pueblos.

When a year later the three priests had not returned, a

wealthy trader named Antonio de Espejo was concerned. So he set out from Santa Barbara to rescue them, following the same route they had taken. But when he reached the Pueblo people and asked about Father Rodríguez and his two companions, Espejo was dismayed to learn that Indians had killed them. He hastened west to what is now Arizona. There he discovered samples of silver ore. Hopeful that the amount of silver here might equal that of (Old) Mexico, Espejo named the area Nueva (New) Mexico. Then he rushed back to Mexico City to apply for a contract to establish a colony in Nueva Mexico.

Spanish law required that to start a colony, one must apply for a contract from the Crown—that is, the Spanish king and his special advisers, known as the Council of Indies. The steps for getting the contract were many and involved. The applicant had to state how many settlers and priests he would take. He had to arrange for their military escort. And he had to agree to help the priests in their work of converting Indians.

Before Antonio de Espejo could wade through all of the necessary steps for getting the contract, he died. In fact, it took so long to get a contract approved that some people did not even bother. A military officer named Castaño de Sosa went north to Nueva Mexico to start a colony without a contract—and he almost succeeded. Then the authorities found out, broke up Castaño's colony, and exiled him to China where he died. Later, two army captains in Mexico deserted their post to go north—only to apparently vanish without a trace.

In 1595, Don Juan de Oñate, a mine owner from Zacatecas, made an offer to the Crown: if they named him governor of the province of Nueva Mexico he would explore this land to the north that no one yet knew very much about. In addition, Oñate promised to pacify (calm) the native people, and convert them to the Catholic religion.

The king and his advisers agreed, and they bestowed on Oñate the title of governor. Although as governor he would receive a yearly salary of 6,000 gold coins, Oñate

Traveling in Style

On Juan Oñate's journey, most settlers limited their personal goods to some clothes, books, and a few dishes and other essential household items. Some soldiers brought very little. When one soldier was asked by a government official inspecting the troops if he had any goods to declare the soldier replied: "I, Diego de Medina, come before your grace and say that I have no arms or other things to declare, except myself, and as this is the truth, I so affirm and swear by God and this cross. Since I do not know how to write, I asked Rodrigo Belmán to sign for me, as witness."

Some officers, on the other hand, had a great deal to declare. One cavalry captain traveled in grand style, bringing 32 warhorses, three suits of armor, a bed, two mattresses and a coverlet, sheets, pillowcases, pillow, and 50 yards of striped canvas for a tent to house himself and his wife and family. Among his many weapons were a silver-handled lance and swords and daggers with handles inlaid with gold and silver. Included in his huge clothing collection were five suits of velvet, satin, or silk with accompanying capes, 12 pairs of boots, 14 pairs of shoes, and three hats, "one black, trimmed around the crown with a silver cord and black, purple and white feathers, another gray with yellow and purple feathers, the third of purple taffeta trimmed with blue, purple and yellow feathers and a band of gold and silver braid."

had to pay for most of the expedition's costs—around a million dollars.

Oñate spent three years making preparations. He signed up 130 soldier-settlers, many with wives and children. And he arranged for the Catholic priests who would hold services along the way and convert the Native Americans once the group established the colony at Nueva Mexico. Among the necessities he bought for the journey were 83 two-wheeled wagons, pack mules and other animals, church bells, guns, tools, spare parts, medicine, and enough food to sustain people and animals for many weeks. Items to trade with the Indians included glass beads, hats, scissors, flutes, and trumpets.

At departure time, the emigrants who were moving from Mexico to settle in Nueva Mexico loaded their personal belongings and the household items they would need onto pack mules. For some of the wealthier officers, several carts were needed to haul their many possessions.

The expedition left the frontier at Santa Barbara in January 1598. Instead of angling northeast to avoid the bleak desert, as earlier explorers such as Father

As the Catholic priests traveled with the Spanish explorers, they put up many crosses. After the soldiers left, many priests — like Brother Juan de Padilla — chose to remain and live among the Indians and convert them.

Search for a Way to the Sea

The early Spaniards in North America knew little about the geography of this new land. Applicants wishing to start colonies had to promise they would search for the "Straits of Anian"—a legendary waterway to the ocean that the Spanish believed was near Nueva Mexico.

Rodríguez and Antonio de Espejo had done, Oñate took a risk. To save time, he chose a route that led straight north even though finding water along the way would be more difficult.

The line of carts and people and animals stretched for nearly four miles. In the lead rode Governor Oñate and the mounted soldiers. Behind them, moving more slowly, rumbled the ox-drawn carts. The drovers—men in charge of driving the animals—waved switches and shouted to keep sheep, goats, pigs, and 7,000 head of cattle from straying. Scouts rode far ahead of the column to search for the best route to follow and, just as important, water.

Locating water in this arid region proved to be a serious problem. The only sources were a few springs and occasional thunderstorms. So if scouts found a river—even several miles off the route—people and wagons halted while the drovers herded the thirsty animals to the river and back.

The going was hard. Over the uneven terrain the two-wheeled wagons slowed to a crawl, especially when they came to the sand dunes. The exhausted oxen nearly collapsed trying to haul the heavy loads across the shifting sand, and sometimes carts and contents had to be abandoned. On a good day, the emigrant train advanced about ten miles, and on a bad day, one or two. When the straggly line of carts and pack animals and exhausted emigrants finally reached the Rio Grande, a jubilant Governor Oñate gave everyone the day off to celebrate.

Carpenters quickly built an altar where the priests held high mass and one of them preached a sermon. Entertainment followed. It began with a play that one of the officers wrote for the occasion. Soldier-actors played the parts. As the action of the play unfolded, the Catholic fathers arrived in Nueva Mexico. Then they baptized the gentle and friendly natives who begged to be converted.

Next, as drums rolled and trumpets sounded, Oñate stepped forward. In a long speech the governor reminded the Spaniards of their duty to convert the native people. Then, in the name of Spain's King Philip II, he claimed the lands of the Rio del Norte and all other lands of Nueva Mexico and all its native peoples. The province of Nueva

Two-Way Trade

Even though law forbade it, caravan operators sometimes crammed all of the supplies for the missions in one section of the wagon train. Then they sold the leftover space to passengers and merchants shipping commercial freight. From Mexico City north the merchants might send coarse wool dress fabric, blankets, jackets, and doublets (outer garments something like vests). Goods shipped from Santa Fe south included painted buffalo hides, antelope skins, candles, pine nuts, and salt that the Indians gathered from dried-up lakes in the desert.

Control Through the Missions

Missions were an important part of Spain's plan for conquering the New World. After the days of the early conquistadores, the Crown realized that killing the Native Americans was not the way to conquer new lands. The colonists needed these native people to work as laborers. So the Crown devised a new way to treat the natives. To make the Indians peaceful and easier to get along with, the Spanish soldiers would first gather them into permanent villages. There the Catholic priests—aided by soldiers—would care for and control the Indians.

The Crown issued detailed instructions on exactly how the priests were to accomplish this. The priests were to convert the Indians—that is, teach them about Christianity and the Catholic religion. The priests were to persuade the Indians to give up their native religions and be baptized as Catholics. Converting the Indians to the Catholic religion had been a major concern of Spain's kings and queens since the Spanish explorers and colonists first arrived in the Americas.

Some crops grown by today's Pueblo farmers are the same as those their ancestors raised— maize (corn), beans, and squash.

For a time the plan worked fairly smoothly. Although some Indians ran away and refused to be converted, many Indians did stay and become Catholics. These converted Indians lived in or near missions where the priests could supervise them. At mission schools and workshops the priests taught them to read and write Spanish, sing, play musical instruments, and practice manual arts, such as weaving, making pottery, working leather, and making wine. Often around the missions were gardens, fruit orchards, and vineyards. Some priests supervised wheat farms, and many had herds of cattle which the Indians tended.

Often, a Catholic priest traveled to outlying areas the Spanish had not yet subdued completely, such as Nueva Mexico and lower California in the west, and South Carolina, Georgia, and Florida in the east. Here the priest often started and ran the mission on his own, without soldiers to protect the mission although usually the authorities provided the priest with food and other supplies.

Mexico included what are now the state of New Mexico and parts of Texas, Colorado, Utah, and Wyoming.

After their day of celebration, the emigrants continued northward. When a mountain blocked their path, advance scouts rode to the east to search for a detour. The scouts found themselves in an arid wasteland where they came close to dying of thirst. The men were saved when someone's dog trotted away, and came back a few minutes later with muddy paws. It had come upon a water hole, the only source of water on the entire 90-mile detour. Later, the Spaniards named this desolate section of the trail *Jornada del Muerto,* or Dead Man's March.

After their roundabout circling of the mountain, people

and vehicles and animals returned to the river. From this point they followed the same path Father Rodríguez had taken 17 years earlier, and Francisco Coronado took 40 years before that. But this time the Indians who met the Spaniards seemed friendlier, offering to sell maize (corn) to the tired and hungry travelers.

Juan Oñate's journey ended in the summer of 1598. It had extended the *camino real* another 750 miles and moved the northern frontier of Mexico to present-day Albuquerque, New Mexico. Once there, the governor's scouts searched for the best place for a temporary capital. They chose San Juan, an Indian village on the Rio Grande River about 30 miles north of the present city of Santa Fe. The people of the village lived in houses made from rock and puddled clay (clay worked with water to a thick paste). When Oñate and the other soldiers arrived, they took over as many of the native people's houses as they needed for their living quarters and offices.

With the help of many Indians, the soldiers dug a ditch to bring water from the river to the village. Also workers began constructing a church large enough to accommodate all the people of the settlement.

The priests started their mission and began to convert the nearby Pueblo Indians to Christianity. Many of the converted came to live at the mission where they worked putting in its orchard and starting a garden. They planted fruit trees, flowers, and grapes, and began to raise melons, wheat, and other products of Spain.

Meanwhile, the governor's soldiers explored surrounding areas. In the plains to the east, near the Arkansas River, they saw buffalo. Closer to San Juan, they visited many Indian pueblos, or towns. In one pueblo, they met two Mexican Indians who had come years earlier with

Castaño de Sosa as he tried to start his colony without a contract. Juan Oñate enlisted the two men as interpreters.

Most Pueblo Indians were friendly—but not so, the Acoma, who lived a ten-day march south and west from San Juan. Their pueblo was perched on a mesa high above a rocky plain, its low houses clustered together. Only one trail led up the steep cliff to the town on top.

In the fall of the year, 30 of Oñate's soldiers came to the Acoma's town. After they got into a dispute with the Acoma over food, the Native Americans killed 23 of the soldiers. To retaliate, Juan Oñate sent a large number of soldiers who conquered the Acoma in just three days. The governor's court in San Juan sentenced each Acoma man who survived the battle to 20 years of forced labor. Then,

Advice from Home Came Slowly

If the governor of an outlying Spanish province had a problem, it might take him a long time to get it solved. For the governor would first have to consult with the viceroy in Mexico City, sending his question by couriers who would travel on horseback on the *camino real*. The viceroy might ponder the question for some time before deciding that the Crown should resolve the issue. Another courier would travel by land and sea to the Spanish court in Madrid, Spain, where the the king and his advisers could spend months—or even years—debating the issue. Eventually, when they decided on an answer, they would send it by a king's representative back to the viceroy in Mexico City, who in turn would send it on to the governor by couriers on horseback, traveling over the *camino real* to the outlying colony.

to discourage any more of what they called "rebellions," the Spanish court ordered that each man over the age of 25 have one foot cut off.

After that, Juan Oñate did not remain Nueva Mexico's governor for long. He was too unpopular with the priests, the colonists, and the officials in Mexico City. The priests objected to the way he treated the Indians. The colonists were angry because they never got the quick wealth Oñate had promised—although there was silver, there were too few soldiers to force the Indians to mine it and the colonists had no intention of working in the silver mines themselves. As a result Oñate wasn't able to provide the Spanish royal treasury with rich ore, and that annoyed the officials in Mexico City. For the only purpose of a colony, in their minds, was to enrich the Spanish royal treasury.

At about this time Spain sent Sebastian Vizcaíno to map the coast of California. (We will hear more about him later.) And in 1607, Mexico's viceroy, the king's representative, advised the Crown to abandon Nueva Mexico and to explore California, instead. In 1609 the Crown replaced Oñate with a new governor, Don Pedro de Peralta.

Governor Peralta's first official act was to move the capital from San Juan to a village in the Sangre de Cristo Mountains. He called the village La Villa Real de la Santa Fe de San Francisco de Asis. Fortunately for mapmakers, the name was soon shortened to Santa Fe.

Santa Fe now marked the northern end of the *camino real*, Nueva Mexico's lifeline to Mexico City. The Spanish royal treasury still paid for the supply caravans that rumbled over the royal road to Nueva Mexico's capital every year or two. The colonists in Santa Fe depended on these goods brought by caravan, as did missionaries, farmers, and ranchers in outlying areas.

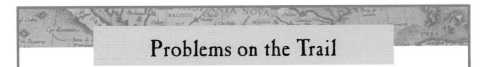

Problems on the Trail

All sorts of problems could delay the arrival of a caravan. Overloaded wagons had to go more slowly. Often they could not cross flooded rivers for many weeks or even months. Broken equipment had to be repaired. Sometimes the men assigned to guard the caravan stole the horses and rode away.

In a contract for a wagon train issued in 1640, the list of spare parts included extra spokes, spare axles, reserve iron tires (each weighing 27 pounds), 500 pounds of tallow (animal fat) to lubricate the wheels, cord to repair the canvas that covered the cargo, and repair equipment such as nails, bolts, hammers, crowbars, and saws.

The caravan operators hauled their supplies in four-wheeled, oxen-drawn wagons, rather than the two-wheeled carts of Juan Oñate's day. Usually 32 wagons made up a caravan. Besides supplies, the wagons hauled mail, royal decrees (orders), and passengers, such as priests, new officials, or northbound settlers.

Beef cattle were herded north with the supply wagons. Some of the cows provided food along the way for people in the caravan, and the rest were given to ranchers in Nueva Mexico. Wagon masters also brought spare oxen for their wagons, and extra parts to make repairs during the six-month long journey north.

By the late 1600s, many settlers became discouraged with life on the frontier. Since there was no wealth to be had and the climate was harsh—too hot in the summer and too cold in the winter—some people returned to Mexico City.

Missionaries had problems, too. Many Indians no longer

respected the teachings of the priests, giving up their Catholic vows and going back to their old religions. Each year, Native Americans working for the colonial farmers had to give the Spanish part of the cloth they wove and the corn they raised as a tribute, like a gift or donation. More and more the Indians came to resent this rule they considered unfair.

The Indians' resentment turned to anger. The anger spread among the pueblos until by 1676 all of the northern pueblos—with the help of neighboring Apaches—had begun to revolt. The Indians did what they could to reclaim their land and force out the Spanish settlers. They destroyed farmhouses and drove the ranchers' horses and cattle into the mountains. In remote country places, they burned churches and sometimes killed the priests.

For the Pueblo people, forcing the Spanish to leave was

Rough terrain at Frijoles Canyon on the Rio Grande was typical of problems along the caravan trail to Santa Fe.

Most Spanish settlements in the Nueva Mexico area were abandoned in the late seventeenth century.

a first step to returning to the way of life and the religions they knew before the Spanish came. To the frightened Spaniards living in Santa Fe or on farms and ranches along the Rio Grande, the rebellion was a disaster. Most of them fled south toward what is now El Paso, a town on the border between Texas and Mexico. The priests who remained in their missions around Santa Fe wrote to the authorities in Mexico City. They pleaded to be sent more colonists and soldiers for protection. By this time, however, to Spanish emigrants the life as a settler in Nueva Mexico seemed too perilous. No one wanted to come. And no more soldiers were sent north, either.

So for 18 years the Pueblo Indians again controlled the land that had once been theirs. Only a scattering of Spanish farmers and ranchers remained in Pueblo land. After 1694 the Spanish reconquered Nueva Mexico, but this time they did not stay long. By the early 1700s, the

authorities in Mexico City gave up for good the idea that
the Spanish might find gold or silver or other rich minerals in the regions to the north. Government officials
withdrew most soldiers from the Nueva Mexico region and
abandoned the military posts.

The handful of Spanish families still living in Nueva
Mexico found themselves with no protection, and nearly
all returned to Mexico. By 1766, the population of Santa
Fe was down to about 200 Spanish people, their Indian
servants, and a few soldiers and missionaries. Although
Santa Fe was still considered Nueva Mexico's capital, El
Paso became Mexico's northern outpost. Lands farther
north, in Nueva Mexico, were left to the missionaries who
had to cope as best they could while the king of Spain
turned his attention elsewhere.

TWO

Florida's
El Camino Real:

The first Spanish explorer to visit Florida was Ponce de León, who sailed to the Florida peninsula from Puerto Rico in 1513 to claim for Spain's king what Ponce believed was an island. He searched for gold, and—some say—for a spring whose waters were said to make old men young. He found neither treasure nor any magical fountain of youth, and left. Soon raiders from the West Indies came to Florida—to plunder the coast not for gold, but for slaves.

Fanciful picture of Ponce de León receiving water from the "fountain of youth."

The Search for Gold

Among the Spaniards who tried unsuccessfully to colonize Florida was Pánfilo de Narváez, who sailed there from the West Indies in 1527. In a short time Narváez and most of the Spaniards who had come with him were dead from accidents, sickness, hurricanes, or Indians' arrows. Among the few survivors was Alvar Nuñez Cabeza de Vaca. After a shipwreck, he washed ashore on Galveston Island in what is now Texas. During the next eight years he wandered across Texas, New Mexico, and Arizona before finally reaching an outpost of New Spain on the Gulf of California. Nuñez Cabeza de Vaca's reports of stories he had heard from Native Americans, about vast treasure and golden cities, spurred the expeditions of *conquistadores* such as Hernando De Soto and Francisco Coronado.

An African slave, Estévan de Dorantes, was one of the few survivors of the Narváez expedition.

In 1521, eight years after Ponce de León's first visit, he returned, this time to start a colony. He brought 50 horses, half a dozen heifers (young cows) and a bull, a supply of seeds, farm tools, and 100 eager colonists. But within six months, hostile natives drove away most of the settlers and killed the rest, including Ponce de León.

Several other Spaniards also failed to establish settlements in Florida, so for a time Spain gave up trying to start a colony there. France had better luck. By the 1560s, French soldiers, civilians—and even pirates—had outposts on the Florida peninsula's east coast.

Having the French so close to Spanish shipping lanes worried Spain's King Philip II. It would be too easy for them to attack his treasure fleets as they sailed by, bound for Spain with pearls and bars of silver and gold from the New World. After a group of French Lutherans known as Huguenots built a fort on the Florida coast, the very Catholic King Philip took action. For not only had these Frenchmen trespassed on Spanish soil—they were Protestants! The king ordered Pedro Menéndez de Avilés to drive the French out of Florida.

On St. Augustine's Day, August 28, 1565, Menéndez arrived on Florida's eastern shore with five shiploads of people and supplies. He brought carpenters, blacksmiths, stonemasons, and other workers and their families as well as soldiers, sailors, and government officials. After

On the eastern shore of Florida, Menéndez established a Spanish fort he called St. Augustine.

establishing a new settlement he called St. Augustine, Menéndez immediately set about his assignment. He and his soldiers massacred any French heretics (non-Catholics) they found. Then they killed the occupants of the French Huguenots' coastal fort—soldiers and civilians alike—sparing only women and children.

From St. Augustine, Menéndez expanded his Florida colony. He sent soldiers to set up a line of log forts as far north as Guale (Georgia) and South Carolina, and as far west as Tampa Bay, on the Gulf of Mexico. Unsure of his geography and the tremendous distances involved, Menéndez made plans to conquer all of the land from Florida to Mexico.

As ordered by his king, Menéndez also set about converting the Native Americans to the Catholic faith. At first, he used soldiers at army outposts as teachers. Later the king sent Catholic priests to be missionaries. Alone or in pairs the priests braved the wilderness. They struggled through dense woods or traveled by canoe to reach groups of native people and establish missions. Sometimes the priests brought dried sprigs of Spanish orange trees, which they planted to begin orchards at the missions.

Each priest followed instructions from the Spanish authorities on how to convert and care for the Indians—some of whom were friendly, and some hostile. First, the priest handed out gifts—bells and caps and bits of ribbon. Then he showed the people religious pictures. When he was able to win the trust of the native people, the priest baptized them and encouraged them to settle near the mission.

Although the missionaries were not allowed to interfere with the decisions of the village elders, they did require their Indian converts to attend church twice daily. Each day the adults worked in the sugarcane fields and fruit

In this 1591 engraving, young Indians train to run endurance races, practice with bow and arrow, and play ball, aiming the ball at a square target in a tree, an early version of lacrosse.

orchards, or watched over cattle herds while the children attended school, taught by the priest. Evening was a time for dancing or games, including a favorite sport with many Indians, a form of lacrosse. At some missions the Catholic priests banned the lacrosse games because the Indians worked themselves into such a frenzy over the sport.

In all matters, the priests were to follow detailed instructions given to them by the Crown. The plan of the king and his advisers was for the missionaries to train the native men to become priests themselves. The Indian priests could then carry on the work in village churches after the Spaniards were gone. The Crown also expected that the converted Indians would be more docile—easier to

The Native American Diet and Farming

A bishop traveling between Florida missions in 1674 described the life of the mission Indians in a letter to Spain's queen. He said the main diet of the native people was hominy, pumpkins, beans, and deer meat. The Indians tended herds and worked the fields together, with the Catholic priests of each village supervising what they did. January was a time to obtain game, and to burn grass and weeds in the fields to prepare them for planting.

train and manage—and more content with their lot. Thus they would be more likely to work for the colonists and to come to their aid in any conflicts with outsiders.

Governor Menéndez dreamed of creating a colony in Florida that could support itself, without depending on help from Spain or the West Indies. With Indians providing the labor, he hoped his Spanish settlers would grow rich. He imagined that they would collect pearls from the sea and minerals from the earth, raise silkworms, and grow grapes, wheat, and rice. Instead, the colony's leader found that there were few pearls around St. Augustine, and not much rich ore. The native people—unlike those the Spanish had converted in other parts of the New World—could not be "tamed." Warriors from the Creek Indian groups refused to till the soil or do other kinds of hard labor. For food and other necessities, the settlers of St. Augustine had to depend on regular visits by supply ships from Havana, Cuba.

The colony's problems discouraged others from coming there. Emigrants from Spain preferred to settle in New Spain (Mexico), where they could get rich while Indians did the work. By this time, the Spanish had also established a colony in Nueva Mexico. But finding settlers willing to come to Florida was so difficult that finally the Crown gave up trying. Instead, Spain came to depend on the missions of a few dedicated priests and a handful of military forts.

By the early 1600s, the priests had established a chain of 24 Florida missions that stretched westward from St. Augustine to Tallahassee. By 1650, there were more than 50 missions in Florida.

As the early priests walked from mission to mission, the paths they followed—often Indian trails that wound through woods and swamps and across rivers and bayous (marshy slow-moving streams)—became Florida's *camino real.* Later this route was sometimes called the Spanish Trail. From St. Augustine, the trail angled southwest

Sketch of how a twentieth-century artist thought the San Luis mission once looked. San Luis was one of the 50 Florida missions established by 1650.

European artist's conception in 1591 of Florida Indians getting gold from a river.

toward the narrowest part of the St. Johns River. Here, two forts guarded the river pass. The road then turned northwest toward the fort at Tallahassee.

Florida's royal road was never used as heavily as the *camino real* linking Mexico City and Nueva Mexico. Rather than take the road, many people in Florida chose to travel by boat between St. Augustine and St. Marks, the port on an inlet of the Gulf of Mexico near Tallahassee. The water route, circling the tip of the Florida peninsula, was safer and easier than going overland.

In 1698 Spain established a permanent settlement and fort in Pensacola, on the gulf coast at the western end of what is now the state of Florida. Gradually the royal road was extended to Pensacola, as Spanish priests started a dozen more missions in northwest Florida—a region called "the panhandle" because of its long, narrow shape, like the handle of a pan.

Year after year the priests continued their missionary work, but over time the Indians often grew restless. Many drifted away from the missions, tired of raising crops simply to feed colonists in St. Augustine. Others went back to religions their people had known before the Spanish came. When the missionaries would not allow the Native Americans to follow their tribal customs, some of the Indians openly rebelled. Often they killed the priests and destroyed their missions.

At the same time, English settlers in South Carolina and Georgia—land that Spain considered a part of Florida—caused trouble of another sort. After 1670 the settlers began coming south to raid Spanish missions in Florida for Indians to work on their plantations. In addition, marauding Creek warriors from Georgia swept down to attack Spanish towns and burn churches. They, too, carried off hundreds of Florida Indians to be sold farther north as slaves. The Creek invaders who took over the area and stayed became known as Seminoles, or Runaways.

Frightened Spanish settlers who lived near missions in the interior fled to St. Augustine to escape the northern raiders. Eventually Spain abandoned most of its inland forts, and permitted only the resident priests to live in mission towns. The priests were given soldiers' pay for defending the towns, but they were not allowed to provide their mission Indians with weapons to help in the defense.

While English and Indian raiders from the north continued to invade Florida, burning missions and taking slaves, another problem was developing for Spain. That was the problem of French trappers and traders in Louisiana who were closing in on Spanish Florida from the west. Because of these threats from the north and the west, Spain's hold on its Florida colony was weakening.

French Louisiana was much larger than today's state of Louisiana. The territory, which the French explorer Robert Cavelier, Sieur de La Salle had claimed for his king in 1682, included all the land drained by the Mississippi River and all the streams that flowed into the Mississippi. This region stretched from Quebec, Canada, to the Gulf of Mexico, and from the Rocky Mountains to the Appalachians.

By the early 1700s, the French had established several settlements in the lower Mississippi River valley. In 1714 the French-Canadian woodsman and trader Louis Juchereau de St. Denis started a trading post at Natchitoches on the Red River about 200 miles north of the Gulf of Mexico. Even earlier, the French had begun settlements on the gulf at Biloxi, Mobile, and New Orleans. These trading posts on the gulf were only a few miles west of Pensacola in Spanish Florida. So Indian and French traders could move easily back and forth between the French settlements in Louisiana and Spanish trading posts at Pensacola. After a time the trails used by the traders became a western extension of the Florida royal road that began in St. Augustine.

Meanwhile farther north, in what is now southwestern Pennsylvania, the English and the French were fighting for control of the upper valley of the Ohio River. The French believed the land was theirs because the Ohio River flowed into the Mississippi River, and the Mississippi and all the streams flowing into it belonged to France. The English felt they were entitled to the land because so many English fur trappers and families had already settled there.

The skirmishes in North America between the English and the French over the Ohio River valley developed into what became the French and Indian War in 1755. France eventually lost the war, despite the help of both its Native American allies and Spain. Following the treaty of peace, in 1763, France gave Canada and all of the French land east of the Mississippi to England. France gave New Orleans and all land west of the Mississippi to Spain. As part of the same peace treaty, England gave back to Spain the Philippine Islands and Cuba—which England captured during the war—and in return, Spain gave Florida to England.

By the early 1700s the *camino real* from St. Augustine, Florida, extended to Louisiana.

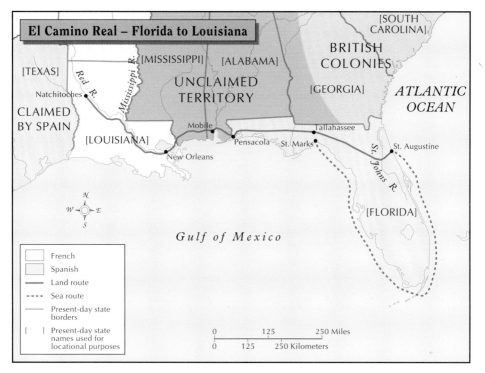

The English divided their newly acquired Florida territory into two parts to make the area easier to control. St. Augustine became the capital of East Florida, and Pensacola the capital of West Florida—an area that included what are now western Florida, southern Mississippi and Alabama, and eastern Louisiana.

English travelers going a short distance to the west followed the Spanish Trail, formerly the *camino real*. Those going all the way to Pensacola from the east usually went by boat—as had the Spanish colonists who lived in St. Augustine years earlier.

In East Florida, the English colonists began to construct a "royal road" of their own, called the King's Road. It extended north and south from St. Augustine, making communication easier for the English colonists in Florida and Georgia. As with those traveling to far west Florida, people who wanted to go up or down the coast went by boat whenever possible. In Florida's back country, English

Naming the Missions

When giving a name to a mission, the early Spanish priests in Florida combined the name of a saint with that of an Indian tribe or area. So among the missions between St. Augustine and Pensacola, there were Concepcion de Apalache, San Francisco de Chuayain, San Pedro de Potohiriba, Santa Helena de Machaba, San Miguel de Asyle, and La Concepcion de Ayabali. Archaeologists today are excavating along what was once Florida's *camino real* to find out more about the early missions, but little evidence remains. For unlike early military structures made of stone or brick, the missions were built of wood that over time has disintegrated.

traders kept to wilderness paths as they met Indian trappers and exchanged their knives and pots for the Indians'
beaver skins.

By the time the English colonies won their independence from Great Britain, in 1783, French traders were
active throughout western Florida and along the lower
Mississippi valley north of New Orleans. Over land, the
traders went by foot or on horseback, and along the many
rivers and bayous they used boats.

After the Revolutionary War ended the English left
Florida, and France again reclaimed the territory. By this
time an active trade route had been established from
Pensacola through Mobile and Biloxi to New Orleans, and
then north to Natchitoches on the Red River. Eventually
the Natchitoches outpost became the western end of the
old *camino real* that had begun in the early 1600s at
St. Augustine on Florida's east coast.

When Spain was again in control of Florida, in the late
1700s, many people rushed south from the United States
to take over the Florida plantations the English had abandoned. At first the Spanish welcomed the Americans. But
as more and more of these foreigners swarmed over the
Spanish territory, Spanish authorities decided it might be
wise to sell out while they had the chance, and so in 1819
Spain sold Florida to the United States.

After that, the Spanish turned their attention to problems farther west, in Texas and Nueva Mexico.

THREE

Spanish Trails
Through Texas

Long after the Spanish had settled parts of Florida and New Mexico, and had even ventured into French-held Louisiana, Spain still had not secured its claim to what is now Texas. Until the late 1600s, this region between the Rio Grande and the Mississippi River remained an unknown country to the Spanish.

Much earlier, in 1519, a Spanish sea captain named Piñeda had mapped the Texas coastline. He did it from his ship, however, and did not go ashore. Nine years later, the Spanish explorer Alvar Núñez Cabeza de Vaca ended up on the Texas mainland—but only by accident, when he was shipwrecked near Galveston. After a grueling 2,500-mile trek Núñez Cabeza de Vaca found his way to Mexico City. There he repeated stories Indians had told him about vast amounts of gold to be found in their lands. His report sent Coronado and Hernando De Soto on separate expeditions that dipped into parts of Texas around 1540. As with other Spanish conquerors, however, the goal of these explorers was to find treasure—not start a colony.

Meanwhile, Mexico's frontier was moved steadily northward, and with it, the *camino real*. In 1609 the royal road reached Santa Fe in Nueva Mexico. But not until late in the 1600s did Spaniards seriously begin to explore the area

Flight South to El Paso

After the Pueblo uprising of 1676, Spanish refugees, Catholic priests, and mission Indians fled south to what is now El Paso, Texas. There in 1682 they founded Mission Nuestra Señora del Carmen. The mission was built by the Tigua, a Pueblo people relocated in the south after the troubles in the north. Today many Tigua people live at the Tigua Indian Reservation and Pueblo at Ysleta, the oldest town in Texas and now part of El Paso.

Nearby, a quiet country road—once part of the *camino real* that led from Mexico City to Santa Fe, Nueva Mexico—connects Ysleta with two other Spanish missions in the Rio Grande valley.

Today, descendants of refugees of the uprisings in New Mexico live at the mission built by the Tigua.

of Texas. When they finally did, they started from El Paso del Norte—a settlement where the northbound *camino real* from Mexico City crossed the Rio Grande.

On June 13, 1684, a few miles downstream from present-day El Paso, army captain Juan Domínguez de Mendoza crossed the Rio Grande into what is now Texas to claim the land for Nueva Mexico. Mendoza did some exploring and was impressed. He hurried to Mexico City where he raved about the abundance of grapes, plums, berries, nuts, and acorns, and of buffalo and other game. Mendoza told of rivers with pearls and mountains full of minerals, and urged the government to send colonists at once to settle what he called the richest land in all of New Spain.

Despite Mendoza's plea, the authorities in Mexico City did nothing. Then, in 1689, Native American traders arrived from east Texas and told of having seen French colonists there. Immediately the authorities sent soldiers to learn if the Indians' story was true. Local native people guided the soldiers to Matagorda Bay, on Texas's gulf shore between present-day Galveston and Corpus Christi. There the Spanish forces found a fort and houses in ruins— apparently from an Indian attack. Later the Spaniards discovered two French survivors of the attack. The Frenchmen told them that the destroyed settlement had been the ill-fated colony of Robert Cavelier, Sieur de La Salle. La Salle, who had claimed the entire Mississippi River valley for France, meant to start a colony at the mouth of the river. Instead, he sailed too far west and landed in Texas.

This news that the French had tried to settle on Texas soil startled the Spanish government into action: settlement of Texas must begin at once—for although this first

In April 1682, La Salle claimed all of the area drained by the Mississippi for France.

French colony failed, there would be others! In the spring of 1690, four priests with soldier escorts departed from Mexico City to establish missions in east Texas and make secure Spain's claim to Texas. The small group headed for the region the Spanish called Tejas, named for the confederacy of local Native American peoples known as the Tejas. During a part of their journey the priests followed the trail taken by the army expedition to Matagorda Bay the year before. Then they angled north and east. The priests started their first mission close to a village of the Tejas on the Neches River, near the present town of Nacogdoches, Texas. Workers laid foundations for San Francisco de los Tejas mission on May 27, and five days later, the priests celebrated mass in their new church. Nearby, they founded a second mission not long after. It was called Santísimo Nombre de María (Sacred Name of Mary).

A reconstruction of the Tejas Mission was built in 1934.

Several months later, Domingo Terán de los Ríos arrived to serve as the first governor of the province of Texas. The trail he followed from Mexico to the missions eventually became a branch of the *camino real* that went north from Mexico City. The Texas royal road was not a single path. Instead, it was made up of several roads that were once Indian paths meandering between Nacogdoches and what is now Eagle Pass, near the Rio Grande. On the Mexican side of the

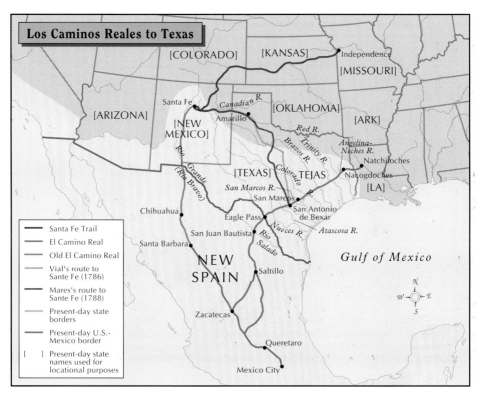

Several branches of the *camino real* led from Mexico to Texas, and from Texas to other points.

river, the Texas royal road joined the *camino real* that connected Mexico City and Nueva Mexico.

Before the new governor settled in Nacogdoches, he continued east to explore the Red River valley in what is now the state of Louisiana. Then Terán returned to establish his governor's office at Nacogdoches. Terán had planned to start a permanent colony in east Texas and build seven more missions, but the grim conditions at the two missions put a stop to his ambitious plans. For a drought had destroyed the crops. An epidemic had killed a great number of the native people, who had no immunity to European diseases. Many Indians who survived refused

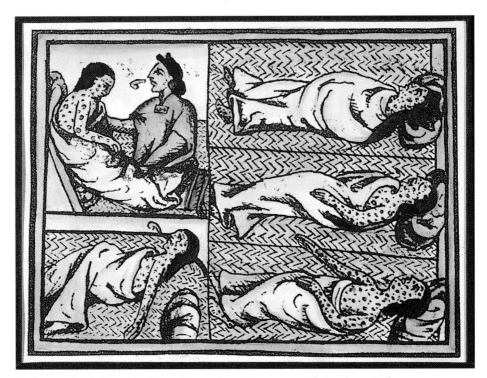

Early woodcut shows Indians dying of smallpox, one of the devastating diseases Europeans brought to the New World.

to convert to the Catholic religion. And often those who did convert left the missions after a time, and went back to their traditional religious practices. A few of the bolder ones even returned to steal mission supplies and livestock.

Things went no better for the new governor. Some of his horses also were stolen. Then a shipment of rice and other supplies from Mexico City did not arrive as expected, making food shortages even more severe. Finally the frustrated governor gave up his plans for establishing a government at Nacogdoches and returned to Mexico.

For a while, the priests struggled to keep the two missions going. It was difficult, because food was still in short supply and even more Indians had run away—tired of the hard work, the strict rules, and the rigid schedules at the missions. Finally, after a flood destroyed one mission, the priests abandoned the other and returned to Mexico in 1693.

For the time being, the Spanish gave up their plan to settle east Texas. Instead, they searched for a new way to keep the French away from Spanish territory. Far to the southwest, on the Mexican side of the Rio Grande that marked the Mexico-Texas border, priests built a mission in 1700. They called it San Juan Bautista. During the next three years, workers constructed two more missions and put up a fort and barracks for 30 soldiers. The fort, called Presidio de San Juan Bautista del Río Grande (Fort St. John Baptist of the Rio Grande), would serve as Mexico's protection against French invaders.

The Spanish had good reason to be worried about the French. In 1682 France had claimed Louisiana—the vast Mississippi River valley that extended west to the Rocky Mountains and east to the Appalachians. In the early 1700s the French established forts where the Mississippi flows into the Gulf of Mexico, at what are now the cities of New Orleans (Louisiana), Biloxi (Mississippi), and Mobile (Alabama). At the same time, the French began to investigate the entire lower Mississippi valley. One of their ablest explorers was the French-Canadian Louis Juchereau de St. Denis. As he trudged through the tangled wilderness and paddled along waterways by canoe, St. Denis got to know the region well. He went west of the Red River, into Spanish territory. This was the same area Domingo Terán de los Ríos visited in 1690, before he tried to start his settlement at Nacogdoches.

While St. Denis was scouting the lower Mississippi and Red River valleys, Louisiana's governor Antoine de la Mothe Cadillac was looking for ways to make money for

Part of the reconstruction of Fort St. Jean Baptiste, one of the forts the French established in Louisiana at Natchitoches.

his colony. Governor Cadillac decided a good way to start was to trade with Mexico. So he sent a ship with French trading goods to Veracruz, Mexico's port city on the Gulf of Mexico. Cadillac hoped to exchange the merchandise for livestock, but to his surprise, officials at Veracruz refused to let the traders ashore. The Frenchmen were told that the Spanish would permit no foreigners and no foreign goods on Spanish soil.

Undaunted, Governor Cadillac devised a new way to trade with Mexico. He would send a trader over land. He chose Louis Juchereau de St. Denis. Besides being both skillful diplomat and able woodsman, St. Denis knew and got along well with the Natchitoche and other Indians of the area, and he understood their languages. Even more important, St. Denis was familiar with the land of the Tejas Indians, which he had visited during his early wanderings farther west.

In late September 1713, St. Denis, with some French companions and several Indian scouts, started up the Mississippi from New Orleans, their canoes loaded with trinkets, axes, hatchets, and other trading goods. Then they crossed over to the Red River, following it northwest until a logjam forced them to abandon their boats. At an Indian village near the present town of Natchitoches, Louisiana, they built a log cabin to store part of the trade goods. Leaving a few men to guard the storehouse, St. Denis and the others started west to begin trading. At villages of the Tejas, St. Denis offered the native people ribbons, knives, cloth, mirrors, and other goods in exchange for their livestock and buffalo hides.

During the early part of his westward journey, St. Denis followed a trail formed by migrating buffalo. The paths ran in fairly straight lines. Sometimes, they were worn as

Buffalo herds such as this migrating east through Tejas (Texas) created the trail that St. Denis followed as he traveled westward to trade.

deep as five or six feet, and wide enough for two wagons to travel side by side. As he walked St. Denis made rough maps of the trail. Farther on, he followed the *camino real* created when the Spanish priests and Governor Terán traveled to east Texas in the late 1600s.

When St. Denis reached Fort San Juan Bautista del Río Grande, on the Texas-Mexico border, he was arrested by Spanish soldiers. They took him to the house of Diego Ramón, commandant (commanding officer) of the fort. The officer politely reminded the Frenchman of Spain's rule: no foreigners and no foreign goods allowed on Spanish land.

St. Denis, equally polite, explained that he had come to the fort on the Rio Grande to buy cattle and other supplies only after he discovered that the Spanish missions in east Texas—where he hoped to make his purchases—had been abandoned.

Commandant Ramón sent St. Denis's papers to Mexico City, where authorities puzzled over what to do next. Meanwhile, St. Denis remained a "prisoner" in the commandant's house—but with freedom to come and go at will. While there, St. Denis and Ramón's granddaughter, Manuela Sánchez, fell in love. After a few weeks, government authorities decided that the French trader St. Denis had violated Spanish law and they transferred him to a jail in Mexico City. By this time, however, St. Denis and Manuela had become engaged. So in his Mexico City jail the Frenchman was treated less as a French invader, and more as the future relative of Commandant Ramón. His jail term lasted only a few months. Then he returned to San Juan Bautista and he and Manuela were married.

St. Denis took up a new assignment—this time working for the Spanish, rather than the French. He guided an expedition of Spanish soldiers and priests who planned to reestablish the abandoned east Texas missions in the Nacogdoches area. Much of the way St. Denis again followed the Texas *camino real.*

One of the priests with the group was Father Francisco Hidalgo, who had helped to found one of the original east Texas missions. As Father Hidalgo took over his duties once more, he greeted some mission Indians he had known 23 years earlier. In the next ten days, the Spanish established three more missions around Nacogdoches. To secure the area against French intruders, they established another mission farther east, on the Red River near what is now Natchitoches, Louisiana—and not too far from where St. Denis had built his storage cabin a few years before. The mission was named San Miguel de Linares de Los Adaes, after the Adaes Indians who lived nearby. Later, the

Try... and Try Again?

Father Margil founded the Mission of Our Lady of the Guadalupe of Nacogdoches in 1716. It was one of four missions the Spanish built in east Texas to form Spain's eastern frontier.

Three years later, eight Frenchmen attacked the mission. No one was hurt, but the Spanish concluded it was wise to leave. They all withdrew to San Antonio for a year, after which the Spanish and the French made peace with one another and the Spanish priests returned to operate their east Texas missions once more.

In 1772, settlers, priests, and mission Indians again had to leave east Texas and retreat to San Antonio—this time, because of the threat of Indian attacks.

Spanish located the new provincial capital of Texas here, calling it Los Adaes.

In 1718, the Spanish founded Mission San Antonio de Valero on the San Antonio River in what is now central Texas. It became a welcome rest stop for weary travelers making the long journey on the *camino real* between northern Mexico and the outpost at Los Adaes. Near the mission a fort went up: Presidio San Antonio de Bexar. A few years later Spain's king sent 15 Spanish families from the Canary Islands to settle in the area and in time the settlement became the town of San Antonio.

Once St. Denis had opened up trade between Mexico and its neighbors, other foreign traders arrived despite efforts of Spanish officials to keep them out. Eventually so many foreigners trespassed onto Spanish land to trade that it became impossible to arrest them all—so the Spanish soldiers stopped trying.

St. Denis moved with his wife to Natchitoches where he started a trading post. He dealt with the local Indians and also made many trips to Mexico City over the *camino real* to exchange shoes, laces, ribbons, silk, and other French-made goods for Spanish hides and silver. In the last years before his death in 1744, St. Denis shipped his goods from New Orleans to Mexico by boat, rather than sending them overland.

In 1763 the lengthy Seven Years War in Europe ended (as did the French and Indian War in North America). As was explained earlier, in the peace treaty, France agreed to give New Orleans and all French possessions west of the Mississippi to Spain. (As a result of the same treaty, Spain gave Florida to England.) No longer did the Spanish in Texas have to worry about the French invading their land. In fact, many French traders in Louisiana simply became Spanish citizens and went on trading as before.

Spain had another more serious worry, however. How could it protect all the frontiers of its vast empire, which now stretched from the Gulf of California to the Gulf of Mexico? The Spanish did not have enough soldiers to do the job and it was costing too much money. And since the priests in the Texas missions found fewer Indians to convert, the attacks on the missions by hostile Apaches, Comanches, Tonkawas, and Wichitas grew more severe. These Indians raided the farms and ranches of Spanish settlers, as well.

Because of all these problems, the Crown issued a royal decree in 1772 ordering the Spanish in Texas to abandon all settlements except those at San Antonio and at La Bahía, about 90 miles to the southeast on the San Antonio River. The capital of Texas was moved from Los Adaes to San Antonio. Entire populations—priests, soldiers, colonists, and mission Indians—deserted missions and settlements in the east to live in San Antonio.

Once San Antonio became the new eastern outpost for Spain, as well as a provincial capital, officials there needed a way to communicate with the other important Spanish outpost and provincial capital, Santa Fe in New Mexico. In 1787, Texas's governor hired French trader Pedro (Pierre) Vial to find the most direct route between the two capitals. Vial established a trail, but it zigzagged too much to suit Spanish officials. So the governor of New Mexico asked José Mares of Santa Fe to do the job. After a couple of tries, Mares found a more direct trail. It led northwest from San Antonio to what is now Amarillo in the Texas panhandle (the area of Texas that juts northward and on a map resembles the handle on a saucepan). From here, the trail went west over the high plains into New Mexico. Then the trail crossed the Pecos River to Santa Fe.

It took Mares three months to make the 810-mile journey. His trail became the official *camino real* between San Antonio and Santa Fe.

Soon after, at the request of New Mexico's governor, José Mares found a direct route from Santa Fe to the busy trading center of Natchitoches, and a few years later Pedro Vial established a route from Santa Fe to St. Louis, a distance of about 1,650 miles. Parts of the trails blazed by Mares and Vial eventually formed a part of the trading route known as the Santa Fe Trail.

By this time, the United States had become a nation, and some of its citizens had begun to move west. The Spanish still controlled much of the southwest, and they imposed strict rules on newcomers. Immigrants who wished to occupy the Spanish land had to give up their original citizenship and swear allegiance to the Spanish king. They were required to obey Spanish laws and accept instruction in the Roman Catholic faith. Often, in order to acquire Spanish land, outsiders took the necessary oath—but did not mean it.

The first land-hungry Anglo-Americans who moved west onto Spanish land crossed the Sabine River to settle in what is now eastern Texas. Even more Americans arrived after Mexico won its independence from Spain in 1821. In the next nine years—from 1821 to 1830—more colonists came to Texas from the United States than had come there during three centuries of Spanish rule.

Because so many Americans were emigrating to Texas, the Mexicans decided to stop the influx in 1830. However, the Texan colonists revolted against Mexico in 1835. In reply to this uprising, the establishment of a Texan government, and the taking of San Antonio by the rebellious Americans, the Mexican dictator General Antonio Lopez

The Alamo

Five Spanish missions were built in the city of San Antonio. The first of the missions, San Antonio de Valero, was a way station on the *camino real* that wound through Texas between the Mexican border and Nacogdoches, seat of the first provincial government of Texas. Later San Antonio de Valero was called the Alamo. During Texas's fight for independence from Mexico in 1836, 189 members of the voluntary Texas army—including Davy Crockett and Colonel James Bowie—died defending the Alamo from attack by over 4,000 Mexicans.

Mexican forces overwhelm defenders of the Alamo.

Antonio Lopez de Santa Anna, the Mexican general, (standing hatless at the center), after the Battle of San Jacinto in 1836, is shown surrendering to Sam Houston (lying on a rug under the tree), who was shot in the ankle.

de Santa Anna sent a large army to put down the rebels. A battle at the Alamo in San Antonio ensued which lasted almost two weeks and resulted in the death of all the Americans inside. Nevertheless, even after this defeat, the Texans continued to fight, rallying to the cry of "Remember the Alamo." On April 21, 1836, they surprised a greater Mexican force at San Jacinto, defeating Santa Anna. Texas had won its freedom from Mexico.

For the next 10 years Texas retained its status as a republic. Finally though, in 1845, Texas joined the United States as the 28th state.

FOUR

Spanish Trails in California

In 1542, Juan Rodríguez Cabrillo, a Portuguese captain sailing under the Spanish flag, entered what is now San Diego Bay in California. He had come looking for gold. Although he found no riches, Cabrillo did take the time to draw a map of the bay—which he called San Miguel.

Continuing north along the California coast, Cabrillo visited the channel islands off present-day Santa Barbara. He discovered Monterey Bay, but missed the narrow opening to what is now San Francisco Bay. On his return south, Cabrillo stopped at one of the channel islands. There he fell and broke his arm. Infection set in and soon after Cabrillo died of blood poisoning.

It was 37 years before another European visited the California coast. He was the English navigator and buccaneer Sir Francis Drake, who beached his ship in an inlet north of San Francisco in

Sir Francis Drake's brief visit to the coast of California in 1579 was made during his three-year voyage around the world in the *Golden Hind.*

1579. Drake stayed only long enough to repair the ship and scrape barnacles from its bottom, and to claim for his queen, Elizabeth I, the land he called "New Albion."

In 1602 Spain reestablished its claim to California when Sebastián Vizcaíno sailed north from Acapulco on the west coast of New Spain (Mexico) to survey and map the California coastline. Vizcaíno anchored in the bay that Cabrillo had called San Miguel. He renamed it San Diego, then continued north as far as Cape Mendocino. When he returned to New Spain, Vizcaíno praised Monterey as the perfect place to start a colony. He told of friendly Indians, wild game, fields of wild grain, and strong timber for construction. He especially noted the excellent bay that was well protected from the wind.

Despite Vizcaíno's glowing accounts, Spain completely ignored California for the next century and a half—though Spanish treasure ships bound for Acapulco from the Philippines sometimes stopped along the coast for fresh water or to make repairs. In the mid-1700s, Spain's attitude toward California changed. Sea otter hunters from Russia were spotted working their way south from the Aleutian Islands, and already Russian vessels were heading toward Oregon. The Spanish feared that the next stop might be California! They also worried that English traders might come overland to California—from Canada in the north, or from the valley of the Ohio River in the east.

Spain had a secure hold on Baja (Lower) California, where Spanish priests had already established a string of missions. But Alta (Upper) California, was a different matter. In 1768, to protect Alta California from what he called "foreign invaders," Spain's King Charles ordered that the region be settled. He appointed a trusted member of the Spanish court, Don José de Gálvez, to carry out the order.

Gálvez planned to do what earlier Spanish colonizers had done: send missionaries and soldiers together. At key points in Alta California the soldiers would build presidios (military forts) for protection and the priests would establish missions and convert the native people. Following Father Kino's system (see pages 62-63), the priests could teach the Indians at the missions useful new skills as well as the Spanish language and Spanish customs. Once these steps were completed, settlers could be brought in.

Gálvez proposed sending expeditions to San Diego by both sea and land. He gave command of the land expeditions to Don Gaspár de Portolá, a nobleman and army officer who had recently become governor of Baja California.

The ships left first. Two passenger vessels sailed from separate ports in Baja California early in 1769. Aboard the *San Carlos* were 23 crewmen, 25 volunteer soldiers, and

The *San Carlos* leaves Baja California, bound for San Diego in 1769. After that voyage, it served as a supply ship between Baja and Alta California and was the first ship to sail into San Francisco harbor.

The Discovery of Father Kino

Eusebio Francisco Kino, Italian-born Catholic priest, came to New Spain in 1681. He had been sent by the Spanish government to help settle Baja California, which the Spanish believed to be possibly the largest island in the world.

Later, authorities gave up the idea of starting a colony in Baja California. Instead, they sent Father Kino to establish missions in the land of the Pima Indians, along the present border between Arizona and Mexico. In all, Father Kino founded 29 missions north and south of the border. The first was Nuestra Señora de los Dolores (Our Lady of the Sorrows), founded in 1687 in Sonora, Mexico, about one hundred miles south of present-day Tucson, Arizona. Here Father Kino lived for nearly 25 years.

The system Father Kino used to start a new mission was always the same—and it was the way his assistant later established missions in Baja California. First, Father Kino visited the Native Americans and gave them gifts. Then he talked about religion and showed them religious pictures. The priest did not try to establish a mission in a village until he felt he had won the people over. Once the Indians were willing, with their help he built the mission. Missions were placed close enough together so that the priest at the new mission could communicate and get supplies from a mission already established.

In 1700 Father Kino founded Mission San Xavier del Bac, just south of what is now Tucson, Arizona. The mission is still in use today.

Full of energy and enthusiasm, Father Kino imported date and fruit trees and started orchards for the many missions he supervised. He taught the Indians how to plant and harvest European grains and raise livestock on their rancherias, or farms. Soon they were producing enough wheat and cattle to send the surplus by ship from the mainland to the missions in Baja California.

Father Kino was also an explorer and expert mapmaker. As he visited the missions spread across his vast parish, he mapped the surrounding areas. Often he made journeys of a thousand miles. He traveled to the Colorado River, and went as far north as the Gila River in the present state of Arizona. During a trip to western Arizona, the Yumas gave him blue abalone shells as a gift. Father Kino recalled seeing such shells on the west coast of Baja California. Yet he knew the Yumas could not have crossed a large body of water to get those shells, so they must have gone to Baja California over land. Suddenly he realized that Baja California was not an island—it had to be a peninsula!

For Father Kino, this meant that instead of having ships bring food and other supplies to the struggling missions in Baja California by sea, mule trains could haul the goods over a land route.

To prove his theory, Father Kino traveled many times to the Colorado River, following it to the river's delta on what is now the Gulf of California. Satisfied that he was correct, Father Kino published a map in the early 1700s showing Baja California as a peninsula. Father Kino even proposed that a road be built between the Mexican frontier on the Gila River and Alta California. But for more than a half century after his death, in 1711, no Spaniards attempted to reach Alta California by land or to start colonies there.

An artist's conception of Father Kino.

one priest. The *San Antonio* carried 26 crewmen, two priests and several carpenters and blacksmiths. Somewhat later, a ship loaded with supplies also departed.

In the spring, the first of the two land expeditions started north from Baja California. The advance guard, led by Captain Fernando de Rivera y Moncado, blazed the trail for the second overland group, led by Portolá, which would leave some weeks later.

In the beginning, the advance group followed the *camino real*, a rough path that connected a dozen missions on the eastern side of the narrow and dry Baja California peninsula. On his march north, Rivera collected small amounts of food and livestock from each mission. Many mission Indians joined his expedition. They carried shovels, picks, axes, and crowbars to hack out a makeshift road once they reached unexplored land beyond the frontier. Rivera depended on the Indian helpers to smooth the way and prevent problems with any natives they met along the way.

With Rivera rode 25 "leather jacket soldiers" (*soldados de cuera*). The name came from their long, sleeveless jackets, made of leather so thick arrows could not penetrate them. The soldiers wore thick leather chaps to protect their legs and thighs from brush and cactus spines, and they carried shields of bull hide strong enough to deflect arrows or spears. The chaplain and chief historian for the advance guard was Father Juan Crespí.

After seven weeks, the advance group arrived in San Diego. Although the two passenger ships were anchored in the bay, Rivera was shocked to learn that it took the *San Antonio* 54 days to find San Diego Bay. And it took the *San Carlos*—which was blown off course—twice as long. All but two of the *San Carlos* crew members had died of scurvy, a disease caused by lack of Vitamin C, and most of

A modern painting depicts Father Serra, Portolá, and members of the overland expedition as they view San Diego for the first time.

its soldier passengers were desperately ill from scurvy or lack of fresh water. The ship carrying the supplies had not been seen since departing Baja California and had apparently disappeared, for it was never heard from again.

On the last day of June, six weeks after Rivera reached San Diego, Portolá arrived. In his group were ten soldiers, 44 mission Indians, and six priests including Junípero Serra, who had been appointed president of the California missions. Portolá immediately sent the *San Antonio* back to Mexico to get new supplies of beans, dried meat, figs, raisins, wine, church bells, and vestments for the priests,

Statue of Father Junipero
Serra at San Diego mission.

to replace those that were lost with the missing ship. Then, only nine days after reaching San Diego, Portolá set off toward the north to find Monterey.

Meanwhile Father Serra, a few priests, and some of the soldiers stayed in San Diego to tend the sick and establish the first California mission. The soldiers quickly built a shelter of grass and mud, and on July 16, 1769, two days after Portolá's departure, Father Serra dedicated Mission Basilica San Diego de Alcalá. The next day, men began work on the fort.

Accompanying Portolá on the march north were Father Crespí and one other priest, seven volunteer soldiers,

Rugged Pacific coast at La Jolla, California, just north of San Diego.

Captain Rivera and his "leather jacket" soldiers, and a number of Baja California Indians. Soldier guards oversaw the pack train of 100 mules loaded with supplies.

Portolá's orders from the Crown were to establish a mission and a fort at Monterey, where Sebastían Vizcaíno had visited 167 years before. That meant heading northwest until they came to the sheltered bay that Vizcaíno had described so enthusiastically.

Whenever possible, the group tried to stay on the coast. Often, however, mountain ranges came down too close to the water's edge.

Present day Highway 101 in California frequently follows the old El *Camino Real.*

Portolá and the others were forced to go inland until they came to a river that might lead them back to the coast again. They were surprised to find that California's rivers did not flow west, but rather flowed northwest, parallel to the ocean. Today's Highway 101 between San Diego and Monterey follows a route very similar to Portolá's.

In his journal, the historian Father Crespí noted that after they camped at a stream near what is now San Juan Capistrano, they felt occasional tremors. The priest named the stream "The River of the Sweet Name of Jesus of the Earthquakes."

When the expedition reached Santa Barbara Channel, they met the Chumash Indians. Watching the native people cutting reeds for baskets or preparing food, Portolá was startled to see them using knives and the worn blade of a Spanish sword—items that the Spanish explorer Cabrillo must have traded to their ancestors 227 years before.

All along the way, the priests had been scouting for good places to establish missions, later on. Father Crespí wrote in his journal that the Chumash of Santa Barbara would make satisfactory converts to Christianity because they were good fishermen, grew a few crops, wore clothes, wove baskets, and had a burial ground.

North from Santa Barbara, Portolá's group found it slow going. Some days, they progressed only two miles. As they approached where Monterey was supposed to be, nothing looked as Vizcaíno had described. He had told of a port sheltered from the wind—but the open bay they had come to was definitely not sheltered. By ship, locating Monterey Bay would have been easy. It was not so easy for men struggling over a rocky terrain thick with brush. Portolá checked his map and studied the sun. Although they seemed to be at the right latitude (distance north or south of the equator), nothing looked right. So Portolá kept going north, thinking Monterey must still be ahead.

The men came to a grove of tall trees of reddish-colored wood. One of Portolá's lieutenants described a tree as hav-

A hut of the Diegueños, an Indian group that Portolá most likely met north of San Diego, drawn by John W. Audubon.

ing "girth so great that eight men placed side by side with arms extended are not able to embrace them." The men, not knowing what these trees were, gave to them the name *palos colorados*, or redwoods. Historians believe this is the first historical mention of the famous California redwood trees.

When Portolá fell ill, he asked his sergeant to continue on north, even though Portolá had calculated they must already have gone too far. Soon the sergeant returned to describe the greatest landlocked harbor he had ever seen—that is, a harbor surrounded and protected by land. The sergeant's discovery of what is now San Francisco Bay meant nothing to Portolá, for he knew that Monterey's bay was definitely not landlocked. Convinced he had failed, Portolá went back to San Diego to admit that he had found nothing.

Father Serra's report to Portolá was no cheerier. The San Diego camp was running out of food, and during the six months Portolá had been away Father Serra had not converted a single Indian. Although the native people gladly accepted his gifts of trinkets and clothing, the priest said they refused to pray or work. He told Portolá that the Indians had stolen everything in sight, even blankets from those who still lay ill. Father Serra said that 50 of the ailing had died and the rest were homesick. Some wanted to give up and go back to Mexico.

Portolá refused to abandon the enterprise. Instead, he ordered Rivera to organize his soldiers for a trip back to Baja California to get needed food. But just as Rivera began his journey, the *San Antonio* sailed into San Diego Bay. Food and supplies had finally arrived; Alta California was saved!

Portolá made a second try at finding Monterey, taking the same trail he followed before. At the same time, the *San Antonio* sailed north with Father Serra aboard. Serra

The Monterey mission, San Carlos Borromeo del Rio Carmelo, situated actually in Carmel, California, as it appeared in the nineteenth century.

and Portolá were to meet in Monterey. Portolá arrived first at the place he had visited once before. But this time he realized that it must, indeed, be Monterey.

Soon after, Father Serra arrived with the ship. Soldiers quickly constructed an altar of branches and on June 30, 1770, Father Serra dedicated Monterey's mission, called Mission San Carlos Borromeo del Rio Carmelo. Above the altar Father Serra placed the image of the Virgin and from a branch he hung two bells. He sang mass, then sprinkled holy water on a huge cross and watched as soldiers raised the cross and fixed it in place. After everyone knelt in prayer before the cross, Father Serra sprinkled holy water on earth, beach, and harbor. Throughout the dedication, a handful of respectful but puzzled Native Americans stood nearby.

Following a brief sermon by Father Serra, Portolá shot off his guns to show that Spain owned this land. Then he ordered his soldiers to begin building a fort of planks and sod, large enough to house 20 soldiers. From the ship, Portolá brought a cannon and other weapons to place in the fort. He appointed one of his officers, Pedro Fages, as acting governor and military commander of California. Then Portolá sailed back to Mexico City on the *San Antonio* to report to the government heads.

In New Spain, the authorities rejoiced. In Monterey, so did Father Serra. So far, he had established two missions— in San Diego, and now in Monterey. And there were more to come. A year and a half later the Monterey mission was

Native Americans being instructed in religion at a mission by a fellow Indian.

moved closer to what is now the town of Carmel, possibly to be nearer fresh water and an Indian village, and farther from the soldiers at the fort. Father Serra lived at this mission until his death in 1784, but he left it often to found other California missions.

By 1772 Father Serra had started five missions. He founded Mission San Gabriel on the Rio Hondo about 120 miles north of San Diego (in what is now the center of Los Angeles). Father Serra named the mission after Gabriel, the angel of good news. Next to be built was Mission San Antonio de Padua, about 50 miles south of the Monterey mission. Then came Mission San Luis Obispo, 70 miles south of San Antonio de Padua.

El Camino Real—"The King's Road"—connected the military outposts at San Diego and Monterey and the missions in between. Although Father Serra had plans for more missions, he had to wait. For authorities in Mexico judged that now it was time to begin colonizing Alta California. To do that, they needed a way to bring in settlers and supplies. Ships were not practical. It was too easy for them to be blown off course, or lost at sea—and there was always the threat of scurvy. Besides, small ships could never carry all of the people and cattle and horses and other livestock required. The authorities realized the only way to colonize Alta California was to have an overland route between the new colony and Mexico.

To build their road, the authorities selected Lieutenant Colonel Juan Bautista de Anza, commander of Mexico's military outpost at Tubac in what is now southern Arizona, between Tucson and Nogales, Mexico. In 1774 Anza organized an expedition from Tubac. With him came a company of 34 soldiers, two priests, cattle, horses, and 35 mules laden with food and other necessities.

Anza's expedition first headed southeast, along a route that dipped into northern Mexico before coming back up to present-day Yuma, Arizona. At the place where the Gila River flows into the Colorado River, Anza managed to cross the Colorado with considerable help from the Yuma Indians who carried all of his baggage. In a Yuma village he met Father Francisco Garcés, who had already explored much of the Colorado River valley. With the priest was a Native American named Sebastián Tarabal who had run away from Mission San Gabriel in Alta California. For a time, Father Garcés and his companion acted as guides for Anza through the desert west of the Colorado River. Despite the help of these able scouts, for two weeks the Anza expedition wandered helplessly among the sand dunes.

Eventually they found a way out of the desert and came to what is now Mexicali, on the border between California and Mexico. From there they angled northwest to the foot of the San Jacinto Mountains. By now, Anza was within 80 miles of Mission San Gabriel, the third of the missions founded by Father Serra.

As soon as the men reached the mission, Anza sent most of his company back to the Colorado River to wait while he and six of his soldiers made a hurried round trip to Monterey. Once Anza had proved that a land route was possible between Mexico and Alta California he returned to Tubac, where his journey had begun four and a half months before. He had traveled nearly 2,200 miles.

In September of the following year, 1775, Anza and his soldiers led the first group of colonists overland to California. The colonists were to establish a town and raise vegetables and other crops to feed the soldiers at the fort in Monterey.

The 30 families chosen as the first California settlers

were very poor. Anza suggested that the authorities pay them in goods, rather than cash. He feared that if paid in money, the men would immediately gamble it all away. So the Spanish colonists were issued guns, horses, saddles, and clothing of all kinds, and the children were given ribbons. Anza took more than 300 beef cattle to provide food for the hungry travelers along the way.

On this second journey west, Anza avoided the harsh desert of present-day Sonora, Mexico. Instead, he went north from Mexico to what is now Casa Grande in

Anza's first and second overland routes west to California. The first route dipped into the Sonora Desert of Mexico. The second followed the Gila River farther north.

Painting done about 1840 of activity around the Santa Clara mission in California.

Arizona. From there, Anza stayed close to the Gila River, following it west to the Colorado River. Again, Yuma Indians helped the Spaniards cross the Colorado safely. At this point, Anza returned to his original trail through southern California.

When the group reached the San Jacinto Mountains, Anza had intended to go straight on to Monterey, bypassing Mission San Gabriel. When he realized how miserable the colonists were, he changed his mind. It was now the middle of December. The weather had turned cold and rainy. The colonists were exhausted, and many were sick. Besides that, already half of the cattle, horses, and mules had died on the trail from lack of food and water. So instead of continuing to the northwest, Anza turned west toward Mission San Gabriel.

The colonists arrived at the mission on January 4, 1776, nearly four months after their journey began. They rested there for a month, and then Anza led them on a three-week, rain-soaked journey to Monterey. Once Anza got the colonists settled, he went north to San Francisco Bay to find the best place to put another fort and mission. The following September the San Francisco Presidio was founded on a hill overlooking San Francisco Bay. Some distance away, Father Serra dedicated Mission San Francisco de Asís in October. A month later, in November, 1776, Father Serra founded Mission San Juan Capistrano north of San Diego.

Soon, more Spanish settlers arrived in California. In 1781, Governor Felipe de Neve and eleven families started a village near Mission San Gabriel. They called it El Pueblo de Nuestra Señora la Reina de Los Angeles (The Village of

A drawing of the pueblo of Los Angeles in 1853.

Our Lady the Queen of the Angels). Before long, residents dropped most of that long name. They kept only "The Angels"—Los Angeles.

In 1782, Father Serra founded his ninth California mission, Mission Buenaventura, halfway between Los Angeles and Santa Barbara near the present town of Ventura. Two years later, Father Serra died, but others carried on his work. Eventually, the Catholic priests established 21 missions in California—each a hard day's walk from the next. The others were Santa Barbara (1786), La Purísima (1787), Santa Cruz (1791), Nuestra Señora de la Soledad (1791), San Juan Bautista (1797), San Miguel Arcangel (1797), San Fernando Rey de España (1797), San Jose (1798), San Luis Rey (1798), Santa Ines (1804), and San Rafael Arcangel (1817). The last in the string of California missions was San Francisco Solano de Sonoma, founded in 1823 about 30 miles north of San Francisco. (Also see the complete list of the California missions on page 78.) Connecting all of the missions along the 600 miles of California coastline was the *camino real.*

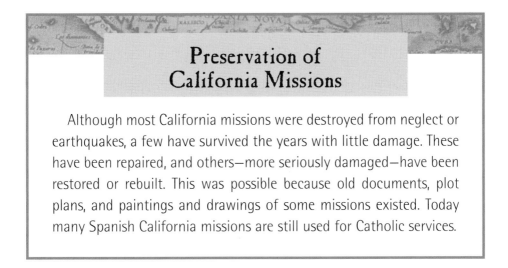

Preservation of California Missions

Although most California missions were destroyed from neglect or earthquakes, a few have survived the years with little damage. These have been repaired, and others—more seriously damaged—have been restored or rebuilt. This was possible because old documents, plot plans, and paintings and drawings of some missions existed. Today many Spanish California missions are still used for Catholic services.

Sites of California Missions

Many California towns grew up on or near the sites of the 21 Spanish missions. At these locations, the remains of missions or mission reconstructions can often be visited. Here are the missions, dates founded, and towns that developed nearby:

1769 - Basilica San Diego de Alcalá (San Diego)

1770 - San Carlos Borromeo del Rio Carmelo (Carmel)

1771 - San Gabriel Arcangel (Los Angeles)

1771 - San Antonio de Padua (King City)

1772 - San Luis Obispo (San Luis Obispo)

1776 - San Juan Capistrano (San Juan Capistrano)

1776 - San Francisco de Asís (San Francisco)

1777 - Santa Clara de Asís (Santa Clara)

1782 - San Buenaventura (Ventura)

1786 - Santa Barbara (Santa Barbara)

1787 - La Purísima (Lompoc)

1791 - Santa Cruz (Santa Cruz)

1791 - Nuestra Señora de la Soledad (Soledad)

1797 - San Juan Bautista (San Juan Bautista)

1797 - San Miguel Arcangel (San Miguel)

1797 - San Fernando Rey de España (Mission Hills)

1798 - San Jose (Fremont and San Jose)

1798 - San Luis Rey (Oceanside)

1804 - Santa Ines (Solvang)

1817 - San Rafael Arcangel (San Rafael)

1823 - San Francisco Solano de Sonoma (Sonoma)

Mission Life

The daily routine was much the same at all of the Spanish missions in California. Converted Indians lived at the missions or nearby, and toiled in workshops forming tiles and adobe bricks, weaving fabric, and making leather saddles and shoes. Spain's goal was to make each mission self-sufficient, with its own vegetable gardens, orchards, vineyards, cattle herds, and grain fields. Although able to produce nearly everything they needed, at some missions the priests traded surplus meat, hides, tallow, oil, and wine for manufactured goods such as furniture, clothing, and tools.

Although the Indians learned many new skills at the missions, for any who were lazy or tried to run away, punishment was severe. Thousands of native people also died at the hands of the Spanish or from European diseases for which they had no immunity. After Mexico won its independence from Spain, Mexican authorities removed the priests from the missions and subdivided the land, turning most of it over to the Indians. Unfortunately many Indians were soon defrauded out of their holdings by unscrupulous settlers.

An artist's drawing of San Antonio de Padua in King City, California

When the Spanish
Were Gone

Long after Spain gave up most of its claims to land in North America, the trails blazed by the Spanish conquistadores, soldiers, priests, and settlers still remained. Americans who came later gave new, non-Spanish names to the royal roads they now took over. They referred to Florida's *camino real* as "Old Spanish Trail." The Texas

Later Trails to the Southwest and California

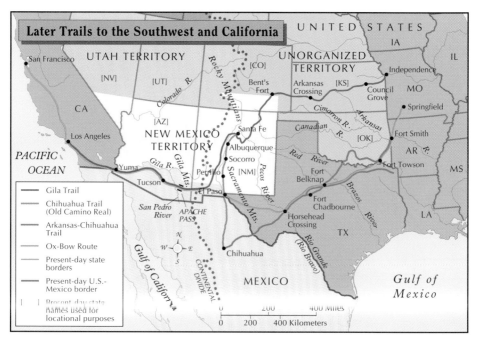

Later Trails to the Southwest and California

camino real became "Old San Antonio Road" or "San Antonio Trace." It was over this trail that Davy Crockett and other Americans came to help Texans in their fight for independence from Mexico in 1836.

In the 1830s, American beaver trappers and fur traders in the West followed what they called "Old Spanish Trail" southwest from the Great Salt Lake area of Utah through parts of Arizona and Nevada to Los Angeles. This trail was an extension of the Santa Fe Trail that came to Santa Fe from Missouri.

Some of the traders and trappers who headed west from Santa Fe went along the "Gila Trail," a more southerly route along the Gila River of Arizona—a route surprisingly close to the one that Father Kino followed more than a century and a half earlier. American traders who brought their wares deep into Mexico traveled the earliest of the Spanish royal roads, the *camino real* that connected Mexico City with Santa Fe. The traders took the Santa Fe Trail from Independence, Missouri, to Santa Fe, and from there went south on the *camino real.* In later years the traders simply passed through Santa Fe without bothering to stop as they went to Chihuahua in Mexico along the "Chihuahua Trail"—as the old *camino real* was then called.

After 1845, when Texas joined the union, many traders bound for Mexico bypassed Santa Fe completely to reach more profitable markets in Chihuahua or Mexico City. Some traders from Arkansas took a shortcut through central Texas on the "Chihuahua-Arkansas Trail." Others followed the "Chihuahua Trail of Texas," which included parts of the Texas *camino real* as it went across the state from Galveston to San Antonio to El Paso. There it joined the main Chihuahua Trail.

In the mid-1800s, some stagecoaches carrying mail and

Modern Marker for Ancient Trail

Florida's *camino real*—later called the Old Spanish Road—led across northern Florida between St. Augustine and Pensacola. Other sections of *caminos reales* stretched over much of the rest of what is now southern United States. In 1929, motorists in St. Augustine formed the Old Spanish Trail Association and set out to follow, as closely as possible, the original Spanish royal roads. After their journey, the Old Spanish Trail Association placed a globe made of coquina—limestone made of shells and coral cemented together—in St. Augustine's central plaza to mark the "zero milestone" of the *camino real.*

Today's U.S. 10 follows portions of Florida's *camino real.*

The globe marking the start of the *camino real* in St. Augustine.

passengers followed portions of the old Spanish trails between Independence, Missouri, and Santa Fe, New Mexico, and between Santa Fe and San Antonio, Texas. Coaches westbound from Santa Fe traveled along parts of the Gila Trail.

To avoid the worst of the winter storms, coaches of one stagecoach company, the Butterfield Overland Stage Company, chose a route that looped far to the south.

The stage for Fort Worth preparing to leave from Yuma.

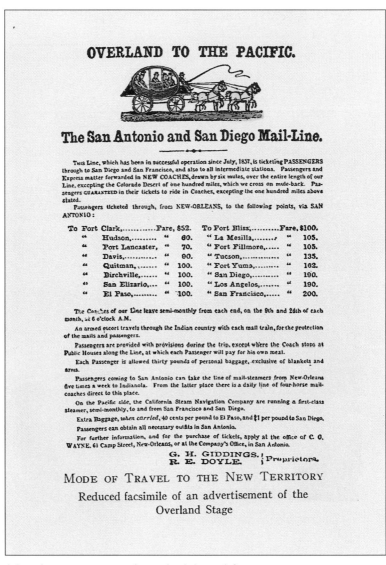

OVERLAND TO THE PACIFIC.

The San Antonio and San Diego Mail-Line.

This Line, which has been in successful operation since July, 1857, is ticketing PASSENGERS through to San Diego and San Francisco, and also to all intermediate stations. Passengers and Express matter forwarded in NEW COACHES, drawn by six mules, over the entire length of our Line, excepting the Colorado Desert of one hundred miles, which we cross on mule-back. Passengers GUARANTEED in their tickets to ride in Coaches, excepting the one hundred miles above stated.

Passengers ticketed through, from NEW-ORLEANS, to the following points, via SAN ANTONIO:

To Fort Clark,	Fare, $52.		To Fort Bliss,	Fare, $100.
" Hudson,	" 60.		" La Mesilla,	" 105.
" Port Lancaster,	" 70.		" Fort Fillmore,	" 105.
" Davis,	" 90.		" Tucson,	" 135.
" Quitman,	" 100.		" Fort Yuma,	" 162.
" Birchville,	" 100.		" San Diego,	" 190.
" San Elizario,	" 100.		" Los Angelos,	" 190.
" El Paso,	" 100.		" San Francisco,	" 200.

The Coaches of our Line leave semi-monthly from each end, on the 9th and 24th of each month, at 6 o'clock A.M.

An armed escort travels through the Indian country with each mail train, for the protection of the mails and passengers.

Passengers are provided with provisions during the trip, except where the Coach stops at Public Houses along the Line, at which each Passenger will pay for his own meal.

Each Passenger is allowed thirty pounds of personal baggage, exclusive of blankets and arms.

Passengers coming to San Antonio can take the line of mail-steamers from New-Orleans five times a week to Indianola. From the latter place there is a daily line of four-horse mail-coaches direct to this place.

On the Pacific side, the California Steam Navigation Company are running a first-class steamer, semi-monthly, to and from San Francisco and San Diego.

Extra Baggage, *when carried*, 40 cents per pound to El Paso, and $1 per pound to San Diego.

Passengers can obtain all necessary outfits in San Antonio.

For further information, and for the purchase of tickets, apply at the office of C. O. WAYNE, 61 Camp Street, New-Orleans, or at the Company's Office, in San Antonio.

G. H. GIDDINGS. ⎱ Proprietors.
R. E. DOYLE. ⎰

MODE OF TRAVEL TO THE NEW TERRITORY

Reduced facsimile of an advertisement of the
Overland Stage

Advertisement announcing schedule and fares
for the Overland Stage.

Called "the Oxbow Route," it began at St. Louis, Missouri, and turned south at Independence, Missouri, then continued south and west to El Paso, Texas. From there it joined parts of the Gila Trail. After reaching Los Angeles, the

Oxbow Route curved north through the Central Valley to San Francisco. Between 1858 and 1861, a trip on the Butterfield Stage Overland Mail from St. Louis to San Francisco covered 2,800 miles and took 25 days.

Unfortunately, travel by stagecoach was dusty, tiring, and often dangerous. Before long, railroads replaced stagecoaches as the preferred way for most travelers to the Far West.

The one Spanish trail that stayed almost intact from the time it was first created in the late 1700s and early 1800s— even keeping the same name—was California's *El Camino Real*. The present California Highway 101, main coastal highway between San Diego and Sonoma (north of San Francisco), still traces the original route of the old royal road that connected the 21 Spanish missions in California.

Glossary

abalone Shellfish with an ear-shaped shell lined with mother-of-pearl; the fish is used for food and the mother-of-pearl is used to make buttons and beads.

Apache Native American group composed of several related peoples living in the southwestern United States.

commandant Commanding officer or officer in charge of a military post or group of soldiers.

conquistadores Spanish conquerors.

convert To cause someone to change from one religion to another; someone who has been converted.

coquina Limestone rock formed of broken shells and coral.

courier One who carries official messages.

Creeks A large group of Indian peoples originally living mostly in Alabama and Georgia.

Crown, the The Spanish king and his special advisers, called the Council of Indies.

drovers Persons who drive animals from one place to another.

el camino real Spanish words meaning "the king's highway" or "the royal road."

emigrant One who leaves his or her home to live elsewhere; in American history, a pioneer who moved westward.

Fountain of Youth Legendary place in Florida whose waters were said to make old people young.

Guale Early name for Georgia.

hawkbells Small, round bells with a metal pellet inside used by Spanish bird trainers to fasten to the legs of hawks used for hunting. Early Spanish explorers and missionaries often gave hawkbells to native people as gifts.

heifer Young cow.

heretic One who disagrees with a religious belief such as the dogma of the Roman Catholic Church; a non-Catholic.

Huguenots French Protestants (non-Catholics) of 1700s and 1800s.

Indians Name given to Native American people by early Spaniards.

Jornado del Muerto Spanish for "Dead Man's March," name given to desolate stretch of land along the Rio Grande north of El Paso.

latitude Distance north or south of the equator.

maize Corn

mission The place where missionaries do their work.

missionary One who undertakes the task of spreading religious teaching.

mule train Mule-drawn wagons carrying goods from one place to another; sometimes called pack train, wagon train, or caravan.

New Albion Land on California coast visited in 1578 by Francis Drake who claimed it for England's queen.

New Spain Early name for Mexico.

notary One who prepares legal papers and administers oaths; known as royal notary when working for a king.

Nueva Mexico A province of New Spain (Mexico) that included what are now the states of New Mexico and parts of Texas, Colorado, Utah, and Wyoming.

panhandle Long, narrow piece of land that on a map resembles the handle of a saucepan.

peninsula A piece of land almost surrounded by water and often connected to land by an isthmus.

presidio Spanish word for military fort.

puddled clay Clay worked with water to make a thick paste; used with rock to make houses.

pueblo Spanish word for town; usually an Indian village in southwestern United States.

Pueblos A farming tribe in what is now New Mexico; the Pueblos at the time of the Spanish occupation were expert weavers and pottery makers.

royal decree Order issued by king or queen.

scurvy Disease caused by lack of Vitamin C.

Seminoles An offshoot of the Creek tribe who settled in Florida in the 1700s.

tallow Animal fat.

Further Reading

Berdan, Francea F. *The Aztecs*. Chelsea House, 1989

Boule, Mary N. *The Missions: California's Heritage* (Vols. 1-21). Merryant, 1988

Cardona, Rodolfo and Cockcroft, James, eds. *Juan Ponce de Leon - Spainish Explorer*, "Hispanics of Achievement" series. Chelsea House, 1995

Chase, John. *Louisiana Purchase: An American Story*. Pelican Publishing, 1991

Crump, Donald J., ed. *Pathways to Discovery: Exploring America's National Trails*. National Geographic Society, 1990

Diamond, Arthur. *Smallpox and the American Indian*. Lucent Books, 1991

Emert, Phyllis R. *All that Glitters: Men and Women of the Gold and Silver Rushes*. Discovery Enterprises, Ltd., 1995

Faber, Harold. *The Discoverers of America*. Simon and Schuster, 1992

Gaffron, Norma. *El Dorado, Land of Gold: Opposing Viewpoints*. Greenhaven Press, 1990

Jacobs, William J. *Cortes: Conqueror of Mexico*. Franklin Watts, 1994

Junipero Serra, "Hispanos Notables" series. Chelsea House, 1995

Lyngheim, Linda. *The Indians and the California Missions*. Langtry Pubns., 1990

Mancini, Richard E. *Indians of the Southeast*. Facts on File, 1991

Morgan, Buford. *Quest for Quivera: Coronado's Exploration into Southern United States*. Council for Indian Education, 1990

Nolan, Jeannette C. *La Salle and the Grand Enterprise*. Marshall Cavendish, 1991

Ortiz, Alfonso. *Pueblo: Southwest*. Chelsea House, 1994

Paulson, Timothy J. *Days of Sorrow, Years of Glory: 1831-1850*. Chelsea House, 1944

Serpico, Phil. *Santa Fe Route to the Pacific*. Omni Pubns., 1988

Smith, Alice. *Sir Francis Drake and the Struggle for an Ocean Empire*. Chelsea House, 1993

Spangenburg, Ray and Moser, Diane. *The Story of America's Roads*. Facts on File, 1991

Bibliography

Blacker, Irwin R. (intro.) and Rosen, Harry M. (ed.), *The Golden Conquistadores*, Indianapolis: Bobbs-Merrill Co., 1960.

Bolton, Herbert E., *The Spanish Borderlands, a Chronicle of Old Florida and the Southwest*, (Chronicles of America Series), New Haven: Yale University Press, 1921.

Carter, Hodding, *Doomed Road of Empire, The Spanish Trail of Conquest*, New York: McGraw-Hill, 1963.

———— *Lower Mississippi*, New York: Farrar & Rinehart, 1942.

Caruso, John Anthony, *The Southern Frontier*, Indianapolis: The Bobbs-Merrill Company, Inc., 1963.

Chapman, Donald E., *Spanish Texas, 1519-1821*, Austin: University of Texas Press, 1992.

Cleland, Robert Glass (edited by Glenn S. Dumke), *From Wilderness to Empire, A History of California*, New York: Alfred A. Knopf, 1959.

Corle, Edwin, *The Royal Highway (El Camino Real)*, Indianapolis: Bobbs-Merrill, 1949.

Crump, Spencer, *California's Spanish Missions*, Corona del Mar: Trans-Anglo Books, 1975.

Davis, Edwin Adams, *Louisiana, the Pelican State*, Baton Rouge: Louisiana State University Press, 1959.

Douglas, Marjory Stoneman, *Florida, The Long Frontier*, New York: Harper & Row, 1967.

Duffus, Robert Luther, *The Santa Fe Trail*, London: Longmans, Green & Co., 1930.

Facaros, Dana and Pauls, Michael, *Florida and Georgia*, New York: Hippocrene Books, 1986.

Florida (American Guide Series), New York: Oxford Univ. Press, 1939.

Gilbert, Bill, *The Trailblazers* ("The Old West" series), New York: Time-Life Books, 1973.

Grant, Bruce, *Famous American Trails*, Chicago: Rand McNally & Co., 1971.

Halleck, Reuben Post, *History of Our Country*, New York: American Book Company, 1936.

Hollon, W. Eugene, *The Southwest, Old and New*, New York: Alfred A. Knopf, 1961.

Horgan, Paul, *Conquistadors in North American History*, New York: Farrar, Straus & Co., 1963.

————, *The Rio Grande in North American History (Vol.1: Indians and Spain; Vol.2: Mexico and the United States)*, New York: Rinehart & Company, Inc., 1954.

Inman, Henry, *The Old Santa Fe Trail (The Story of a Great Highway)*, New York: Time-Life Books, 1981.

Kocher, Paul H., *California's Old Missions*, Chicago: Franciscan Herald Press, 1976.

Lavender, David, *The Southwest*, New York: Harper & Row, 1980.

———, *Westward Vision, The Story of the Oregon Trail*, New York: McGraw-Hill, 1963.

Louisiana, (American Guide Series), New York: Hastings House, 1941.

Moorhead, Max L., *New Mexico's Royal Road: Trail and Travel on the Chihuahua Trail*, Norman: Univ. of Oklahoma Press, 1958.

Morison, Samuel Eliot, *The Oxford History of the American People*, New York: Oxford Univ. Press, 1965.

National Geographic Editors, *Trails West*, Washington, D.C.: National Geographic Society, 1979.

Norworth, Howard, *The Pathway of the Padres*, Los Angeles: Shield-Way Publishing, 1951.

Ormsby, Waterman L. (Only Through Passenger on the First Westbound Stage), *The Butterfield Overland Mail* (edited by L.H.Wright and J. M. Bynum), San Marino, Calif.: The Huntington Library, 1960.

Patton, Phil, *Open Road*, New York: Simon & Schuster, 1986.

Pindell, Terry, *Making Tracks*, Weidenfeld, N.Y,: Grove, 1990

Riesenberg, Felix, Jr., *The Golden Road, The Story of California's Spanish Mission Trail*, New York: McGraw-Hill, 1962.

Rister, Carl Coke, *Comanche Bondage*, Lincoln: University of Nebraska Press, 1989.

Skates, John Ray, *Mississippi*, New York: W. W. Norton & Co., 1979.

Snell, Tee Loftin, *The Wild Shores: America's Beginnings*, Washington, D.C.: National Geographic Society, 1974.

Sprague, Marshall, *The Mountain States*, New York: Time-Life Books, 1967.

Sunset Editors, *The California Missions*, Menlo Park, Calif.: Sunset Publishing Co., 1991.

Time-Life Editors, *The Old West, The Pioneers,* New York: Time-Life Books, 1974.

———, *The Spanish West*, New York: Time-Life Books, 1976.

Waitley, Douglas, *Roads of Destiny, The Trails that Shaped a Nation*, Washington, D.C.: Robert E. Luce, Inc.

Winther, Oscar Osburn, *Via Western Express & Stagecoach*, Stanford, Calif.: Stanford University Press, 1945.

Young, Stanley, *The Missions of California*, San Francisco: Chronicle Books, 1988.

Index

Note: Page numbers in italics indicate maps; numbers in bold indicate illustrations.